MY COLLEGE TIPS

WALDENHOUSE

Walden, Tennessee

MY COLLEGE TIPS

written by a college student for college students

by James S. Parker

WALDENHOUSE

Walden, Tennessee

COVER ARTWORK: designed by Quantal Langford. COVER LAYOUT: designed by James S. Parker

MY COLLEGE TIPS written by a college student, for college students!

Published by Waldenhouse Publishers, Inc.
100 Clegg Street, Walden (Signal Mt.) Tennessee, 37377 USA
888-222-8228   www.waldenhouse.com
Printed in the United States of America

Library of Congress Cataloging-in-Publication Data

Parker, James S., 1977-
   My college tips : written by a college student, for college students! / by James S. Parker.
      p. cm.
   ISBN 0-9705214-5-6 (pbk. : alk. paper)
   1. College student orientation. I. Title.
   LB2343.3.P27 2000
   378.1'98--dc22

                              2004016471

CONTENTS

SPECIAL THANKS TO:

- *Hassin Dean, Pamela Henry, and Aaron Duffy for proof reading and reviewing the rough draft of this book.*

- *Nick Hartline, for his expertise in Fraternity life.*

- *Dr. Kittrell Rushing for being a great professor and reviewing this book.*

- *Dr. Ellen J. Neufeldt for taking time from her busy schedule to sit down with me to review this book.*

- *Karen Stone for being so patient and guiding me through the publication process.*

- *My wife, Kalee, for proof reading the final version of this book.*

- *My friends and family for their love, support, and belief in me.*

- *Our Lord for his many blessings.*

- *And, all the professors, faculty, fellow students, co-workers, university administration, and employers that influenced my college experience in every way. Without you, this book would not have been possible.*

Message from the Author

Greetings future college graduate. There are a number of reasons that you may be reading this book. Maybe you received it as a high school graduation gift, or perhaps you have decided to gain a little insight for your path through the college world from someone who has recently been there. Regardless of your personal situation, you are interested in attending college. Well, congratulations! College is a big step into the world of adulthood. You will accomplish something that many people don't even want to try. College is a learning experience. Not to mention, when you get your degree, you will increase your salary potential, job security, and professional status. Everyone's college experience is different. What you make of it is up to you.

This book is a guide to help you start your college career. I made many mistakes in college, and I am putting my lessons learned out there to help others. You can choose to learn from them, or ignore them. The choice is yours, but always remember the number one tip I am trying to express with this book is to "Keep trying, and never give up." When you fail, try again. Many people that start college encounter obstacles and just give up. Keep trying and put forth a good effort. You can do it.

My goal in writing this book is to provide you with a roadmap to success in both the academic and personal world. The tips reflect my own personal opinion, based on the experiences I had throughout my 8 years of college. The tips are numbered for reference only and do not have rank associated with them. With the purchase of this book, you gain special login privileges to the accompanying website at www.mycollegetips.com. Please feel free to visit www.mycollegetips.com for further explanation on tips, helpful links, student gifts, and other college-life related topics. I hope that you find this book useful and that you take a few things away that will benefit your college experience. Who knows, you may even graduate faster than I did!

Good luck and best wishes,
James S. Parker

www.MyCollegeTips.com Login Information
User ID: student
Password: mctbjsp#03

FAMOUS COLLEGE QUOTES

- The things taught in schools and colleges are not an education, but a means to an education. - *Ralph Waldo Emerson*

- The college undergraduate is a lot of things - many of them as familiar, predictable, and responsible as the bounce of a basketball, and others as startling (and occasionally disastrous) as the bounce of a football. - *John Sloan Dickey*

- I have never let schooling interfere with my education. - *Mark Twain*

- The first two years of college are vocabulary lessons. The second two years are spent learning who to ask and where to look it up. - *Bill Austin*

- Colleges are places where pebbles are polished and diamonds are dimmed. - *Robert G. Ingersoll*

Top ten reasons I am qualified to write this book

1. 8 years of college
2. 5 different colleges
3. Changing majors numerous times
4. Moving 2000 miles away to go to college
5. Student Loans and Scholarships
6. Personal and financial difficulties
7. Relationships and social life
8. Jobs and money
9. Living away from home
10. Finally getting my degree

1. From High School to College
Reasons to go to college

1. *To get the piece of paper* – To earn a degree to make your future more secure.

2. *To gain valuable personal and professional experiences* – You will change while in college, usually for the better.

3. *To mature* – You're a legal adult now; it's time to start acting like it.

4. *To have the time of your life* – College life consists of so many activities that you will find intriguing.

5. *To meet your potential life long partner* – There are different students in each of your classes every semester. You may be sitting next to someone you could develop a lasting relationship with.

6. *To get out of the house* – Get out of your parents' house; learn some independence.

7. *To meet new people* – Make friends, professional contacts, and see #5.

8. *To challenge yourself* – If it were easy, everyone would do it.

9. *To learn who you are* – We go through so many identities while growing up. Your time in college is when you stop trying to fit in so much and be yourself.

10. *To do something that most could not* – You could be the first to get a college degree in your family.

THINGS EVERY HIGH SCHOOL STUDENT SHOULD DO IF THEY WANT TO GO TO COLLEGE

1. *Research potential schools* – Do they offer the degree you are interested in? What is the school's reputation? What does it cost? What is the school itself like?

2. *Take the SAT/ACT early* – Start taking it as a junior, and if you don't do well enough you have plenty of time to increase your score. Don't wait too long to take the test or you might miss out on admission to the college of your choice.

3. *Do the best you can in high school* – From experience, I should have tried to make better grades in high school. You can qualify for more scholarships and grants if you do. I have a friend who was our valedictorian, and he got so much scholarship and grant money that he had some left over for semester spending money.

4. *Save money* – It is nice to have money saved to help you through those first couple years of college. Start putting a little every week into a savings account. That money could buy you a spring break getaway to Cancun.

5. *Send out as many graduation announcements as possible* – Many relatives and friends will send you money for your graduation. Save it! See #4. You may even receive money from relatives you have never met before. Don't forget to send thank you cards.

6. *Apply for scholarships* – Even if you barely meet the minimum qualifications, try. It is worth a little effort to possibly gain some free funding for college.

7. *Apply for financial aid* – Just by filling out the FASFA, you may find that you qualify for a grant and/or loan.

8. *Check out work study programs* – This is a nice way to work your way through college if you and your family don't have the funding.

9. *Visit campuses and talk to current students* – Current students will tell you much more information than any brochure or admissions counselor.

10. *Believe in yourself* – Even if no one in your family encourages you or finds it necessary. You can do whatever you put your mind to.

THINGS ANY HIGH SCHOOL STUDENT SHOULD KNOW BEFORE GETTING TO COLLEGE

1. *You're starting over with a clean slate* – If you go to a college in another city, people don't know you, what you did in your past, or that you have changed because of the past. By the time you get to college, you have learned a lot about yourself and how you want people to see you. This is your chance to start fresh. Don't screw it up!

2. *College is better than high school* – People are more mature. You can go to parties and social interactions.

3. *No matter how much money you have saved up, it will not be enough* – Between impulse buys, new credit cards, and tuition increases you will not have enough money for the entire year. Get a job or keep that scholarship because you are going to need it. Hey, there is always mom and dad!

4. *You will have to study more* – Topics are harder, pressure is higher, and you want to keep that scholarship; but don't stress too badly. Remember you get to choose the classes.

5. *You are not the big fish on campus anymore* – Don't wear your high school letterman jacket and don't act like you are the star. Remember there are probably at least a hundred other star quarterbacks and prom queens that are also freshmen.

6. *Expect to not get the classes you want at the times you want them* – Being a freshman means you get last pick on classes. Your best bet is to beat out the other freshmen that have procrastinated. Go through orientation as early as possible, and register for classes to get the best possible schedule.

7. *It is okay to be roommates with a good friend* – Take it from me. I roomed with one of my best friends, Tom, and we had our fights but we became better friends and could depend on each other.

8. *Consider going to a community college first* – Especially if you're not sure of what you want to study. It is significantly cheaper, classes are smaller, and you can get your general classes out of the way.

9. *This is college not high school; grow up!* – Don't do the immature things you did in high school like pick on the nerds or make fun of the ugly girls. You might need the nerds to help you in a class, and that ugly girl in high school might be a future supermodel.

10. *Expect the hassles* – Expect to wait in long lines, fill out numerous forms, need many signatures, show proof of this and proof of that, and to run around campus because your school didn't put the financial aid records office and admissions office in the same building. Oh, most important, expect to receive the wrong information and wrong dates from some of the school staff.

TOP THINGS TO CONSIDER BEFORE GOING TO ANY COLLEGE

1. *Is the department you want to enter accredited?* – Ask the dean of the department of your choice. Non-accredited departments receive less funding which means fewer classes, fewer instructors, and fewer options. Also, many employers and graduate schools require a degree from an accredited school.

2. *What is the faculty like?* – Are they understanding, helpful, and well-spoken instructors? Is the instructor's accent so thick you won't be able to understand his/her lectures? It is also a pain when a professor is not willing to help the students and understand our learning habits. Every student is different. We all learn differently.

3. *How is campus life?* – Are there activities, sporting events, clubs, and recreational facilities? You may not want to go to a school that doesn't have a football team, basket ball team, or an activity of your interest.

4. *Consider the surrounding area to the college* – Are there cool places to go within walking distance? Are conveniences such as grocery stores, laundromats, gas stations, and Wal-Mart (Ok K-Mart can do too) available within a reasonable distance?

5. *Check out the city itself* – Is it a college town or does no one support the school? Would you want to live there if the school was not there?

6. *Check out student services* – Are there tutoring, employment, medical, and other services offered on campus. If there are not many helpful student services, then the college obviously does not put its students first.

7. *Is it worth the amount of money?* – Some people spend too much money because they are either from out of state or it is a private institution. Try getting in-state tuition after going to a community college first; then transfer. If you are considering a private college, is it really worth the money you are spending?

8. *Is the school too big or too small?* – Some schools have so many students that you could have 100 people in one class. Or, some colleges are so small that you have the same 15 people in every class. Decide which is right for you or consider a school in between.

9. *What is the school's reputation?* – It is one thing to talk to the admissions staff. You know they will talk the school up. Go out and talk to the actual students and get the real low down.

10. *Geography of the school* – Is it too cold or too hot for you? Is it too far from where you want to live? Would you rather go to a school in the mountains or near the ocean? Choose a place that will make you happy.

2. GOING TO COLLEGE

TOP HELPFUL TIPS TO SUCCEEDING IN COLLEGE

1. *Go to class* – Even if your teacher does not have an attendance policy, show up. Professors recognize whether or not you put the effort into attending. I attended every class of my most difficult courses, and still do not know how I received a 'C'.

2. *Get to know the faculty* – Go to your professor's office to ask a question about the material and possibly lead into other conversations. The professor sees you putting effort in and you will find it easier to engage in class discussions. It helps for the professor to know what kind of person you are.

3. *Determine your major within the first 2 years* – During the first two years of college, you take most of the general classes like English, Math, History, Economics, and more. Take a couple of classes related to majors you are interested in. If you like them, you can choose that major and still graduate within a reasonable amount of time.

4. *Use your college resources* – Take advantage of tutoring services, computer labs, libraries, and more. These resources can make it much easier on your class assignments and understanding of the material.

5. *Study* – This is a given. Unless you are going to remember everything from every lecture, you need to put time into studying.

6. *Don't procrastinate* – If you are given a project that is due in a month start as soon as possible. I have had incidents where I waited until the night before to write a paper and the next morning when it was due the printer died on me. I was not allowed to turn it in late.

7. *Enjoy college life* – You are on your own now; you go to class; you do your homework, and you study. Now go out and have a safe but great time.

8. *Stick to a major* – Once you choose a major, try to stick with it. If you realize you detest the major you have chosen, research other majors that require some of the classes you have taken already.

9. *Don't change schools* – This may sound crazy, but I learned this the hard way. The same major/degree at two different schools can require completely different classes. If you change schools, it can set you back one whole year or more.

10. *Find a punching bag* – I don't mean to go out and buy a punching bag. College is stressful, so relieve that stress when you have it built up. Go out with friends, go play ball, workout, or hit that "bag" as hard as you can.

THINGS TO TAKE TO COLLEGE

1. *Clothes* – Take necessities. Jeans, shirts, shorts, jacket, athletic shoes, casual/dress shoes, sandals, a few nice outfits, sweats, bathing suit, workout clothes, undergarments, socks, hats...you get the idea.

2. *Transportation* – Car (if you have one), bike, roller blades, skateboard, or other.

3. *Music* – Boom box, CDs, portable CD player with headphones. Music is great to study to or to listen to while hanging out with new people in the dorm.

4. *A Few Fun Items* – Guitar, playing cards, football, basketball, volley ball, board game.

5. *Personal Hygiene Products* – Shampoo, soap, deodorant, tooth brush/paste, razor, shaving cream, and more. No one likes a smelly roommate.

6. *School Supplies* – Pens, pencils, erasers, paper, notebook, planner, calculator, index cards, tape recorder, markers, highlighters.

7. *Pictures* – Bring some pictures of your friends, family, and girlfriend or boyfriend. Don't over do the pictures. Creating a shrine of your girlfriend/boyfriend will cause people to think you are a bit obsessed.

8. *Camera* – You will meet so many new people and do so many cool things. Take lots of pictures to remind you of the great times you had.

9. *Address Book* – To keep up with your family and friends while at college and to record new friends and contacts.

10. *Miscellaneous* – Towels, sheets, bedspread, pillow, cups, water bottles, aspirin/pain reliever, sunglasses, phone card, bean bag, laundry basket.

THINGS NOT TO TAKE TO COLLEGE

1. *Too many clothes* – You have a limited amount of space. Bring only the necessities, and ladies, that does not include 15 pairs of shoes.

2. *Toys* – Keep the distracting stuff at home, like the Playstation or Nintendo. Remember, you are there to study. Besides, you are likely to meet someone who brought their own video game system.

3. *Computer* – Chances are that your school will have a number of computer labs available to students that will have Internet access, printer, and all the programs you will need. Bringing your own computer might be more of a pain than a convenience.

4. *Television* – Again, this is another distraction. Most dorms have a couple of TVs in a local student lounge area anyway.

5. *Anything not allowed in the dorm* – There are certain restrictions to items that you may possess in a dorm. They could create fire hazards, like a hot plate or toaster oven. Check the student handbook for items that are restricted.

6. *Mom and Dad's Credit Card* – This can get you in a lot of trouble financially.

7. *Valuables* – Don't bring a bunch of jewelry, collectables, or anything that can't be replaced easily. There are many cases of theft that occur in dorms.

8. *Childhood Keepsakes* – Stuffed animals, letterman's jacket, baby blanket, or other items that will make you look childish or immature.

9. *Room Decorations* – For now, don't worry about buying and bringing a bunch of decorations because you want your room to look cool. You will have time to find ways to decorate your room that will be much cheaper.

10. *Large Items* – Don't bring large items like a fridge, couch, chair, large stereo system, or anything that won't be useful.

THINGS NOT TO DO IN COLLEGE

1. *Drugs* – All illegal drugs are bad. That is the reason they are illegal. Even marijuana, which most people deem harmless, can be a gateway drug to things that are much more harmful. It affects everyone differently. Some get sick, some feel no effect, and others get addicted. Why find out how it will affect you? Just don't try it. Not to mention, it affects your brain and you lose a lot of what you have learned in school.

2. *Party all the time* – Have fun, but be responsible. Remember what you are there for. Your goal is to earn a degree.

3. *Be a drunk* – No one likes a drunken fool. I have been down this path and, trust me, everyone does stupid things while under the influence of alcohol that they regret later.

4. *Date your roommate's ex* – This will cause a lot of tension. There are plenty of other men or women out there you can date.

5. *Lose touch with good friends* – I hate it when this happens. I had some great friends in high school that completely changed and they ignored me in college. However, I still keep in touch with some friends even though they live 2000 miles away. Don't lose touch; you may regret it.

6. *Spend money on unneeded things* – My first year of college, I got two credit cards. My spending went out of control. I bought black lights, lava lamps, posters, stereos, CDs, party favors and more. Don't buy this junk. Buy the necessities and ask for the junk as gifts.

7. *Sleep around* – Sex is a special thing. I know how that sounds, but it is. Emotions and feelings are strong in something so intimate. Some people take this for granted and go on sexual rampages. STDs are too common and reputations are too fragile. Remember, it is not a bad thing to keep your virginity.

8. *Take out too many student loans* – I learned this the hard way. You think, *All right, free money!* Well, you eventually have to pay it back. If you do take out more than one student loan, try to use the same lender/bank. It will help when you consolidate all your loans when you're out of school.

9. *Rebel against everything* – No one wants to be around someone that disagrees with everything all the time.

10. *Waste your time by not wanting to be there* – You have to want to go to college. Even if your parents make you, don't "show them" by flunking out. Try to find something that you like.

THINGS THAT WILL LEAD TO YOUR DOWNFALL IN COLLEGE

1. *Cheating* – Not doing your own work will hurt you in future classes because you didn't learn the material. Cheating can also get you expelled!

2. *Getting in debt* – A lot of debt could force you to concentrate on paying bills when you should be concentrating on school.

3. *Substance abuse* – Tobacco, alcohol, prescription drugs, and illegal drugs can cause problems in your social life and school.

4. *Lack of motivation* – If you are not motivated, you will not enjoy college; you won't enjoy your classes and you may lose the motivation to get your degree.

5. *Not being self-reliant* – Having your mom do your laundry on trips back home does not make you self-reliant.

6. *Stressing out* – Stress and college go hand in hand. Keep it under control and don't let it consume you. Stay on top of your classes and your finances. As long as you try your best, that's all anyone can ask.

7. *Losing your funding* – Do everything you can to keep your scholarship, grant, or any other financial aid you may have received. Don't lose it by getting bad grades or some other issue you could have controlled.

8. *Lack of direction* – Pick a college and a degree by the end of your 2nd year of college. Changing majors and/or schools too many times will waste class credits and prolong your eventual graduation.

9. *Breaking the law* – Don't make stupid decisions to break the law. You may jeopardize your scholarship, grant, loan, your freedom, or even potential employment.

10. *Having Sex* – Conceiving a child or worse, contracting a sexually transmitted disease, will change your life. Remember, even "protected sex" is not 100% safe.

CHOOSING A MAJOR OR MAJORS

1. *Do something you like* – If you study something that you enjoy, you are more likely to complete your degree and succeed in your career.

2. *Do something you're good at* – If you have no idea what you want to do, go with what seems easiest to you. It is better to have any kind of degree than none at all.

3. *Double major in business or pick up a minor* – If you choose to be a business major, it would be extremely useful to double major. It would only be about 8 to 10 extra classes (depending on the school) and you would have two degrees. Or, choose a minor. For example, a student majoring in marketing could minor in graphic design and broaden their potential.

4. *Choose something that the economy will need in the near future* – Research what the future outlook is on specific jobs you may be interested in. Concentrate on the positions that have an increase in number of jobs available.

5. *Choose any major to get that piece of paper* – A degree shows a potential employer that you are educated, self-sufficient, self-motivated, and dedicated. This can lead you to jobs in several fields of work.

6. *Visit your school's career center* – Most schools offer a career guidance office where you can get counseling and even take a career test.

7. *Choose a major based on potential salary* – Decide how much you would like to make. If salary is not as important as other criteria, go with what makes you happy.

8. *Research potential career interests* – Most schools have a career center where you can research job markets, future career outlooks, salaries, and more.

9. *Decide how long you are willing to spend in college* – If you want to be a college professor, then you will spend around 8 to 9 years in college. But a high school teacher usually only requires a 4 year degree.

10. *Find the best fit major* – Gather what classes and credits you have and find a degree that would use most of those classes.

Tips that no school official will tell you up front

1. *Petition for all possible credits* – Every school has a board made up of faculty and staff that looks at a student's classes that he or she has taken and decides if they get credit for a transfer course. If you do not get immediate credit for a transfer course and you think it is equivalent to the course at that school, then fill out a petition for credit in the records office.

2. *Do not take classes you won't need* – Only take extra classes if they are needed for a prerequisite or you need extra hours to remain a full time student.

3. *Go by your original catalog year* – If you started college in 1999, and it is currently 2005, go by the 1999 catalog year. Sometimes the requirements change and you would have to take extra classes should you change catalog years. Stick to the original one and it may save you a class or two.

4. *You can get that scholarship* – If you think you can't get a scholarship because your GPA is too low, think again. Scholarship committees look at other criteria like major, financial need, extra curricular activities, and more. So just try; the worst that could happen is to be denied.

5. *Don't take your advisor's word for it* – Many advisors do not stay on top of new graduation and transfer requirements. Look them up yourself; talk to other students, or ask a teacher you trust to confirm what you've been told.

6. *Don't assume school officials want to help you* – You are just another student name on their list, and they may not want to go out of their way to help you. You may have to insist that they work on what you need.

7. *The hidden requirements* – Make sure you know as much as possible about the requirements for your classes, scholarships, loans, and graduation requirements. Advisors will not always tell you what you need to do.

8. *Deferred Tuition Payments* – Some schools allow you to defer your tuition payments over a period of time. Watch out for an additional fee to use this option.

9. *You can petition your grade* – If you receive a 'D' in a class you thought you got a 'C' in, don't just accept it. Petition the grade to make the professor look back over your scores. Who knows? You may have received someone else's grade by mistake.

10. *You don't have to be considered full-time for student loans* – Many students don't know you only have to be half-time to qualify for student loans and/or defer your loan payments. The system may lead you to believe you have to keep full-time status at all times.

3. Money, Jobs, Budgeting & More
Helpful financial tools while attending college

1. *Government-issued student loans* – FASFA Federal student loans are convenient because just about any student can get one. You don't pay anything while in school and no interest accumulates until after you graduate. The interest rate is usually lower than any other loan.

2. *Scholarship* – Research all types of scholarships and apply for any for which you meet the minimum qualifications. Free money is worth your time!

3. *Government Grant* – By filling out a FASFA form every year, it is always possible to receive a Pell grant or other free aid. Even if you don't qualify, it is the same form you are required to fill out to receive a loan.

4. *Your parents* – If your parents can help you, great, but don't take advantage of their generosity and get kicked out of school, fail, or drop out.

5. *Yourself* – By paying for classes yourself, you have less accumulated debt when you graduate and you will appreciate the fact that you supported yourself through college. Let possible employers know that. There is a respect factor there that people who had a free ride don't earn.

6. *A job that pays you and pays for school* – Many employers offer tuition reimbursement, book money, and other money. Find one and take advantage. See page # 45.

7. *Your savings account* – Maybe you have saved up your allowance or birthday money for the past 8 years. Well, it's time to finally make a withdrawal from that savings account!

8. *That rich uncle you hardly talk to* – If you have a wealthy relative that is willing to front you the money, then great! Offer to pay them back after you graduate, or you could just attempt to become their best friend.

9. *Your significant other* – If your significant other truly cares and has the means, then they should be more than willing to support you. As you read this I am paying my wife's way through college.

10. *Your credit cards* – This is a last resort source of funding. When no other option is available use it. Make sure you pay at least the monthly minimum payment.

GOOD JOBS TO HAVE WHILE ATTENDING COLLEGE

1. *Server* – Make cash on every shift; easy to pickup a shift; nights and weekend shifts fit well into a school schedule.

2. *Internship/Co-op* – These are usually great for professional work experience; they usually pay well; and they understand that school comes first.

3. *Anywhere that pays your tuition* – Work for a company that you can get tuition reimbursement. It might pay a little less than another job, but the benefit is worth it.

4. *Work-study program* – These programs are usually arranged through your school. Look to sign up for one and get paid to study.

5. *Legal assistant/secretary* – I have never had this job but have known people who have. Good pay; good experience; and you can do homework or study at work when not busy.

6. *Anywhere that gets you experience in your field of study* – If you are a graphic design major, take a cheap paying graphics job that will look good on your resume. Remember, it is not enough these days to simply have a degree; employers look for experience also.

7. *Lifeguard* – Great summer work; tan; fun; and nice change from the daily school-year grind.

8. *School computer lab assistant* – Make sure people sign into the lab; help them out when needed; but best of all, get paid to do your homework.

9. *Self-employment* – Set your own hours and reap the benefits of success. If you fail, try something else. If you couldn't sell your custom designed t-shirts to local students for a profit, switch gears and start doing lawn service, or see page 42.

10. *Dorm residential assistant* – Free stay in your own room with meals provided. Down side, you have to bust the freshmen every once in a while and it makes you look like a jerk.

TIPS TO LAND A JOB AT THE INTERVIEW

1. *Be yourself* – Don't act like someone else to try to get the job. It is better to be yourself upfront so they know if you will fit into their work environment.

2. *Be Prepared* – Research some quick information about the history of the company, where the company currently stands relative to their market, and what you can offer to your job should they employ you.

3. *Dress Appropriately* – Find out how employees dress at the company and dress the same or just above that level. When in doubt ask the secretary.

4. *Strike up a conversation* – Ask about the job or the company. Be sincerely interested in what they are taking about.

5. *Be Confident* – Act like you will be getting the job. It makes them more hesitant to reject you.

6. *Don't Be Cocky* – Don't be over-confident or this could give the sign that you are condescending. No one likes arrogance.

7. *Smile* – A smile can say a lot about a person and even put someone in a better mood.

8. *Make eye contact* – This shows that you are listening and interested. If there is more than one person conducting the interview, make occasional eye contact with each person.

9. *Talk about positive job experiences* – When asked about something you have done specifically in professional work, tell them about any positive experiences. Don't ramble on about how John didn't pull his weight so you had to work overtime. Who is John and who cares?

10. *Ask questions about employment* – Ask things like: When would I be able to start? Will I receive any training? Who will I be working with? This shows the interviewer that you are truly interested and you will gain even more information about the job.

TOP BUSINESSES TO START WHILE IN COLLEGE

1. *Lawn/Yard service* – Buy a cheap lawnmower and some hedge trimmers; then pass out some flyers around your neighborhood.

2. *Website* – Sell a service, product, or advertising.

3. *Textbook buy and sell shop* – Start a little shop near campus selling used books back to students and buying theirs when the semester is over.

4. *Sell your own art* – Sell your artistic creations to others. Why wait until after college if people want them now?

5. *Baby sit or nanny* – If you can handle other people's kids, go for it! Sometimes you can even live with a family for free rent. Ever seen "Charles in Charge"?

6. *House cleaning service* – Buy a vacuum cleaner, mop, and a towel and pass some flyers out in an upscale neighborhood.

7. *Mobil car detailing* – Let it be known that you are available to go to a customer's house to clean his/her car.

8. *Clean windows* – Easy, no-brain work. Grab a bucket, towel, and squeegee and go to local businesses to ask if they need their windows cleaned.

9. *Paint houses and/or pressure wash* – Just get the equipment and post some flyers.

10. *Sell your own service* – If you learned to do graphic design or build a website, try to go out and get some clients interested in your service. Remember you can undercut the competition by offering lower prices for quality work.

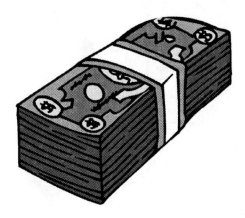

44

COMPANIES THAT OFFER OR HAVE OFFERED COLLEGE TUITION ASSISTANCE

1. Bank of America

2. Sears

3. TGIFridays

4. YMCA

5. State Farm Insurance

6. Bell South Communication Systems

7. Capital One Financial Corp.

8. Coors Brewing Company

9. Dupont

10. General Electric

WAYS TO SAVE MONEY FOR BOOKS/TUITION/ SPRING BREAK

1. *Buy/Sell textbooks on Internet* – A campus bookstore will rip you off. Buy your textbooks online and save a lot of money. You can even profit from it when you buy textbooks you need from other students on campus and sell them back online.

2. *Don't be an impulse buyer* – One of the first things I did my first year of college was buy a stereo system, high tech VCR, black light, lava lamp, mountain bike, and the list goes on. Point being, I moved back home after that school year with 2 credit cards with a $1500 balance and a bunch of junk.

3. *Buy necessities first* – If you know you have a $250 car payment to make next week and you have the money now, don't go buy a car stereo you just saw on sale.

4. *Buy the generic brands* – Natural Light Beer and Wal-Mart brand bread, chips, crackers, pasta, and peanut butter will save you big in the end.

5. *Dedicate a percentage of your paycheck to a broke fund* – Deposit a percentage of each paycheck into a savings account you never use and save it for emergencies such as finals week, spring break, or an unexpected fender bender in the parking lot.

6. *Drink water instead of a soft drink or tea* – When you must go out to eat, order water. It saves at least a dollar every time you do it, and don't forget to tip your server.

7. *Don't splurge* – If you know you need milk, but don't drink it very often, buy a half gallon instead of a whole gallon.

8. *Donate plasma* – I never did it but I know people who did, and it was extra money in their pocket. I have a needle phobia.

9. *Make a budget and stick to it* – If you know you can spend $20 a week on food, then don't spend a penny more. At the end of the month you may have a little extra dough saved up to take a date to a nice restaurant.

10. *Get a roommate* – I have gone through many roommates and, if you are a tolerable person, this can put extra money in your pocket and cut your utility expenses in half.

PLACES TO GO FOR A CHEAP BUT FUN SPRING BREAK

1. *Anywhere you have family* – The good thing about family is that they want to see you and you can stay for free and even eat for free sometimes. You may be able to choose between an aunt that lives 20 minutes from Ft. Lauderdale, or your grandparents that live an hour away from 3 ski resorts in Colorado.

2. *Go camping* – No hotel room fees, cheap food, plenty of drinks, and some of your best friends sitting around a campfire.

3. *Wherever you go, drive and carpool* – Driving is a lot cheaper than flying. When you carpool, you save even more by splitting the gas bill with your friends.

4. *The local spring break area* – Most schools have a place that is relatively close and cheap for a good spring break getaway. Talk to other students and find out where it is.

5. *Take a tour of a resort club* – Some resort clubs that want people to join will give you free night stays, food, and offer other incentives just to take a 90-minute tour of

their resort. This works in your favor but remember to stand up against the pressure when the sales pitch comes.

6. *Go with a club on spring break* – I have had some friends that were in clubs such as a kayaking club, a scuba diving club, and others. Most of these clubs plan a trip to do the activity they like best at group rates.

7. *Use the Internet to find vacation packages* – Check out www.travelocity.com or www.expedia.com to find package deals to places on the beach or a cabin on the mountain of a ski resort. Book the trip early to save more money.

8. *Go on a trip with your church* – Good clean fun and worthwhile.

9. *Stay in town* – Do things in town you normally don't do but have always wanted too. "Hey I didn't know we had hang gliding and rock climbing!"

10. *Go Home* – Go visit your parents and your friends back home. Free stay, free meals, rest, and relaxation.

4. Social Life and Dating
Ways to improve your social life

1. *Get a job* – This is the easiest way to meet people by far. Just work in a place that has employees close to your age. Within that work environment, you have to talk about work, but that talk may lead to social talk.

2. *Talk to people* – In class, ask a fellow student about something you might have in common, such as a major or another class. Most people are a little more at ease when the other person has made initial contact. Next time they might talk to you first.

3. *Hang out with anyone of the opposite sex* – It is a proven fact that men and women form tight friendships. Even if you don't find yourself attracted to that person, they have friends too.

4. *Start a club* – If you enjoy a sport or activity that others also enjoy, you might offer to start a club.

5. *Don't try to date the first person you meet* – Make friends with as many people as you can first. Then meet their friends and their friends' friends. Too many people

rush into a relationship with the first person that shows interest in them, and they miss out on excellent opportunities.

6. *Be available* – When a social opportunity arises, make yourself available unless it absolutely conflicts with a prior engagement. Saturday night dinner with Mom can be put on hold for one night.

7. *Call people back* – When someone calls you and leaves a message, the polite thing to do is to call them back to acknowledge their call, even if you must decline something they may be inviting you to.

8. *Don't overwhelm the social contact* – When you first meet someone and they invite you out, do not take advantage of their friendliness by calling them everyday or trying to hang out with them constantly. You want them to know that you can get along without them.

9. *Be yourself* – Even if some people don't like you, be yourself. There is always someone that you can have a friendly connection with.

10. *Smile* – You let people know you are approachable when you smile.

Reasons to join a Fraternity or Sorority

1. *Social Contact* – When joining a Fraternity or Sorority, you will meet many people through every aspect of Greek life.

2. *Opportunity for Service* – You will have the opportunity to volunteer and take part in many activities that will benefit your school and other groups.

3. *Study Help* – Fraternities and Sororities require their members to maintain good grades. They provide tutors and study sessions for members.

4. *Professional Contacts* – You will meet other members that you will form close relationships with. Those close bonds will continue into your professional career. You start networking as soon as you join. Remember, it is not always what you know, but who you know.

5. *Develop Communication Skills* – Being engaged in numerous activities will improve your skills. You may be a shy and bumbling freshman when you first join, then the social coordinator during your senior year.

6. *Organized Events and Trips* – Spring break trips, dances, and socials are some of the organized events that are a lot of fun.

7. *Further your career* – Many Fraternities and Sororities are formed from specific majors, career goals, and other criteria. By joining, you will meet others with very similar career paths and will become involved in activities that will provide you with professional experience.

8. *Added Benefits* – There are many other things that you may gain from joining a Fraternity or Sorority. (i.e. scholarships, jobs, an alternative place to live, and more.)

9. *New Resources* – If you join a Fraternity or Sorority, you can use the resources that would not be available to you otherwise. You have the ability to accomplish things that you might not accomplish on your own. Colleges give certain privileges to Fraternities and Sororities that they would not give to an average student.

10. *Diversity* – By joining you are forced to deal with diversity. This is a positive thing, especially if you do not come from a culturally diverse background.

Reasons not to join a Fraternity or Sorority

1. *You have to pay* – You must pay dues. The amount of dues you are required to pay can vary, but being in a Fraternity or Sorority is not free.

2. *It can be time consuming* – A Fraternity or Sorority can be very time consuming. They require a certain amount of service and time devoted to study. I have lost good friends because they spent all their time with their Fraternities.

3. *It may not be beneficial* – You may already have a great social life and are involved in many activities.

4. *You are not into the experience* – You may not want to go through Rush or any of the extreme activities that Fraternities and Sororities are involved in.

5. *People can be fake* – In the beginning, men and women can be very misleading about what kind of people are in their Fraternity or Sorority. If you join the wrong one because of false first impressions, you could end up in an unfavorable situation.

6. *You want to establish a social connection on your own* – You may feel that by joining a Fraternity or Sorority, you don't truly make friends on your own. You may feel that you are told who to be friends with.

7. *You have to follow a new set of standards* – Fraternities and Sororities have rules that must be followed like certain number of hours of studying per week, amount of service, and other required participation to become and remain an active member.

8. *To party* – You should not want to join a Fraternity or Sorority just to party. This is the wrong motivation to have going into it. Sure, there will be good times, but they require much more out of you than just partying.

9. *You are not up for the responsibility* – Joining a Fraternity or Sorority is a lot like a job. You have many responsibilities that you must keep up with. This can be difficult especially if you have a heavy class load and a real job.

10. *You become what the Fraternity or Sorority wants you to become* – You may never find out who you really are naturally because you were expected to act certain ways to fit in with the Fraternity or Sorority.

WAYS TO MEET PEOPLE

1. *Live on campus* – Roommate, roommate's friends, neighbors, neighbor's friends; it is a list of endless possibilities.

2. *Get a job where other students work* – At work, you are forced to interact with other employees. Ask some other employees to go hang out after a night of hard work.

3. *Get involved with school-related groups* – Join a club that you have an interest in like kayaking, soccer, drama, or start your own.

4. *Go to church and attend functions* – Many campuses have church functions on or near campus. Go and see if it is right for you. If it is, get involved.

5. *Form study groups in classes* – Be the one in class to form a study group for a big exam coming up, then play the gracious host.

6. *Take a class for the sole purpose of meeting people* – I have done this. Take something that is interesting to you such as weight lifting, scuba diving, or Art 101. Make sure it is a class where there is a lot of interaction.

7. *Be outgoing* – Smile, say "Hi, my name is…" Ask them how they are doing in class.

8. *Volunteer* – Find a way to help someone else out. You will meet good, caring people.

9. *Go out, even by yourself* – This one is tricky. No one wants to go out by themselves. We fear that people will look at us as loners or losers. Suck it up and do it. It will work out. Just be yourself and see #7.

10. *Workout at the gym* – Start playing basketball, volleyball, or working out. When you have done it enough, you will begin to recognize other people that come as often as you. Time to be outgoing.

Top ways/places to meet the potential love of your life

1. *Work* – The down side is if it does not work out, you still have to see this person.

2. *Church* – You already share one very important similarity.

3. *Class* – A great way to talk to that attractive person next to you is to form a study group and invite them.

4. *Friend of a friend* – This is a classic method.

5. *Introduce yourself* – Not to everyone. But there are times in our lives when we connect with someone else in a situation such as class, at the mall, gas station, or anywhere. You look that person in the eyes and you both might be having a moment. You never know if this could be the person or not, so introduce yourself.

6. *Your sister's/brother's friend* – Your family knows you best and knows what kind of person you like. Well, maybe not your parents.

7. *At a place you enjoy your favorite activity* – You already have that activity in common, now strike up a conversation and go from there.

8. *In the same dormitory/apartment complex* – Scope out that person you have wanted to talk to and do your laundry the same time they do theirs. Unless you don't want them to see your underwear, "yet".

9. *Throw a party* – Hey, it is your house, your entertainment, go meet everyone you don't know already. Remember # 4, friends of friends.

10. *Update your look* – If you are still wearing that run down high school sports jersey, consider buying new clothes. Check out stylish magazines to keep up with changing looks.

THINGS TO AVOID IN THE DATING WORLD DURING YOUR COLLEGE YEARS

1. *Conflicting religions* – This is a large issue for two people who have strong religious beliefs that conflict.

2. *Dating someone just for the way they look* – Wrong thing to do. In the long run, looks won't matter anymore and someone is going to end up hurt.

3. *Avoid dating someone in a fraternity or sorority if you are not in one* – It is hard to date someone that is in a fraternity or sorority simply because they are so involved in it that you end up being number 2 on their list of priorities.

4. *Dating someone because they are the top jock or popular* – Remember this is not high school anymore. Personality is more important than stature.

5. *Dating someone that just broke off their 2 or more year relationship* – You will be the rebound person and it might be fun for a week or two, but chances are they go back to what they are familiar with or they decide they want to play the field.

6. *Someone just like you* – I can't explain this well but experience shows opposites attract.

7. *Those really attractive people you put on a pedestal* – If you really feel that this person is your dream girl/boy then you will never be yourself. You will go out of your way to make them happy and you won't be happy.

8. *Avoid being the cheatee* – Don't be the person that someone cheats on their significant other with.

9. *Don't date someone just because he or she is easy* – If you heard that this person is "easy," then there may be other surprises you don't want to find out about. Besides, you shouldn't date someone just because you heard a rumor about them.

10. *Avoid dating someone that you wouldn't want to bring around your friends* – This is just plain wrong. You may lead this person on thinking everything is fine when the whole time you have been keeping them out of the loop. Do the person a favor and break it off so they can find someone that will appreciate them.

TIPS FOR MEN REGARDING WOMEN

1.   *Have women friends* – It is ok to have women friends. If you do, the chances are better of you meeting more women through them and maybe meeting the one you have been looking for.

2.   *Be a man* – Most women like the old-fashion style of dating. You know, the man arranges the date; the man picks up the bill; the man opens the door, and the man initiates the good-night kiss.

3.   *Take care of your personal hygiene* – Take a shower daily, wear deodorant, cologne, brush your teeth, and keep the body hair under control.

4.   *Be a nice guy instead of a macho jerk* – Times have changed since high school. Most mature women are not into that chase anymore. In college, the macho jerk is out.

5.   *Control the bad habits* – You know what I mean. Do I have to spell it out? Just ask any woman what bad habits men have.

6. *Compliment women* – Women can be insecure with their looks, clothes, body, and more. By complimenting her, she feels better about herself and she realizes you notice her.

7. *Don't check out other women while on a date* – Big no no, if you plan on going on a second date.

8. *Don't talk about your ex-girlfriend when you are on a date* – Even if she was a great girl or the worst, just leave her out of the discussion.

9. *When a woman talks to you, don't assume she likes you romantically* – But don't put it off to the side either. Just follow her lead.

10. *Forget about the pickup lines* – Try to find a common interest to talk to a woman about and approach her, "Hi, my name is …."

TIPS FOR WOMEN REGARDING MEN

1. *Be the aggressor sometimes* – Some men find it very appealing when a woman is the aggressor. Surprise him and make the first move.

2. *Stop fishing for compliments* – If a man is a gentleman and he takes interest in you, he will compliment you. Confidence is an excellent trait.

3. *Don't talk about your ex-boyfriend when you are on a date* – The same thing goes for the guys. Most guys don't want to hear about the ex-boyfriend.

4. *Be happy with your appearance* – It is a downer when a woman is always unhappy with how she looks. Strut your stuff and be proud of who you are.

5. *Stop asking "Do I look FAT!"* – You really don't want the truth to that anyways.

6. *Understand that a man is a man* – Bad habits, stupid actions, and wrong comments are a given. Please, forgive us.

7. *When a man talks to you, don't immediately think that he is hitting on you* – Let him down easy if you are in a relationship only when you know he is pursuing you

romantically. Otherwise, just be friendly in conversation. Some men really do want to be "just friends."

8. *Be straight forward* – I am not saying that guys are always strait forward, but in most cases the man asks a woman out. Don't beat around the bush and say you are washing your hair on Friday night if you're not. Honesty is an admirable trait.

9. *Express what you are thinking* – Men don't always pickup on subtle signs that women send. If he is not reading the signs, then help him out; just tell him what you want.

10. *Don't put all men in the same category* – All men are different. If you had a bad experience with one, don't assume they will always be the same.

GETTING ALONG WITH YOUR GIRLFRIEND

1. *Open the door for her* – Makes her feel special.

2. *Compliment her* – Women like to hear that you pay attention to their looks, style, and other things worthy of a compliment.

3. *Don't be overly possessive* – I have not met a woman that says she likes overly jealous guys.

4. *Treat her like a lady* – See #1 and #2.

5. *Show affection in public* – Hold hands, small kisses, and hugs.

6. *Value her opinion* – Many times, women think differently from men. It is another way to view something that you may not have thought of.

7. *Listen to her* – Sometimes a woman needs to talk about something so she'll feel better. Sometimes it has nothing to do with you. Just sit, listen, and be supportive.

8. *Don't overwhelm her with stuff* – Don't buy her too many things, or say I love you too soon.

9. *Surprise Her* – Buy her a flower every once in a while or surprise her with a special date.

10. *Say "I am Sorry"* – Even when you think you are not wrong.

GETTING ALONG WITH YOUR BOYFRIEND

1. *Don't nag* – This reminds us of our mother telling us to take out the trash.

2. *Give him time with the guys* – There are times when men need to act stupid. Call it testosterone if you want but we have a guard up that needs to be let down around the guys. If you think about it too much, it is just confusing.

3. *Be supportive of what style he has* – Just because we don't wear belts that match our shoes does not mean we don't have feelings, too. Clothing, decorations, and accessories are not as important to men as they are to women. So help us when we really need it. Don't say, "You are not going to wear that out with me!"

4. *Scratch his back and he will rub yours* – Most guys are not flexible enough to scratch their own backs and women have nails.

5. *Cook him a good dinner* – I know it is traditional but it is always nice to know that a woman can cook.

6. *Be the initiator sometimes* – A man likes it when a woman takes the initiative in setting up a date, giving a kiss, or other things.

7. *Don't try to control him* – No one likes to be controlled. Even if he does, his friends and family will notice and they won't like you.

8. *Don't degrade his manhood* – If he treats you like a lady, then he deserves the same respect.

9. *Don't try to completely change him* – There are some things that men do just because they're men. Most of us don't mind a little change to make you happy, but don't expect to raise him like your own puppy dog. Ever heard the saying "You can't teach an old dog new tricks?"

10. *Be straight forward instead of giving mixed signals* – "Is there anything wrong?" "NO!" Remember, men and women think differently. If you are upset about something, let him know what it is. He probably doesn't know what he did. Most of us know that you do this on purpose to torture us. Don't make us apologize for something we have no idea about.

5. ROOMMATES
TOP ROOMMATES TO HAVE

1. *A friend that you know you can live with* – A friend that has similar interests and has similar living habits.

2. *A sibling* – You have already grown up in the same house, so why not split the rent if you haven't killed each other by now?

3. *Someone of the opposite sex* – Just as friends. Sometimes it is easier to get along with the opposite sex.

4. *Anyone that is willing to split the rent and actually pay* – Any honest paying roommate is good. Their bad habits are minimal when money and valuables are at stake.

5. *A cat* – Furry, soft, lovable, self-sufficient, and easy to live with. Cats are more acceptable to landlords than dogs are. Just make sure to keep the litter box clean.

6. *The person you want to marry* – Try to see if you can live together before you get married. This will answer a number of questions you may have with your relationship.

7. *A fraternity brother or sorority sister* – You both will have similar schedules and activities.

8. *A teammate* – Not only will you be practicing and traveling together, you can help each other work on your game.

9. *Someone that you might learn something from* – Maybe they are a better student or posses a good social life. Stick around and feed off them to be stronger in areas where you are weak.

10. *A spoiled kid* – This may sound shallow but you can reap the benefits of the roommate being spoiled by his/her parents. They may have the cool stereo, big TV, and furniture. Be careful in case mom and dad cut them off though.

Roommates to Avoid

1. *Your best friend* – If you think you can't live together, don't. It could ruin a friendship that is more important than finding a roommate.

2. *Someone from a different culture* – Too many clashing differences from cooking to cleaning may be hard to live with.

3. *Your mom* – Grow up. It is nice to have Mom do your laundry and make meals but you don't have real freedom.

4. *Someone that you work with* – You see them at work and at home. You may need a break every once in a while.

5. *Someone with a child* – I know this sounds insensitive. But you may eventually have your own family. Give yourself a chance to have fun in college. Think about what would go on if you lived there. Crying baby; baby sitting; can't stay up late listening to music, etc.

6. *Puck from "The Real World"* – Crude, dirty, insulting, selfish, and inconsiderate. No positive aspects to a roommate of this kind.

7. *Someone who has a criminal record* – Red flag. Ask for a $1000 cash deposit, and they don't get it back if they steal from you or miss a rent payment.

8. *A person that completely conflicts with your personal schedule* – You might need to study on Friday nights. Don't get a roommate that will be hosting a party on Friday nights.

9. *Someone that you would like to date* – This is a bad reason to get a roommate. Chances are that you will not date and it may cause tension by living together.

10. *Someone that is not from your generation* – It is likely that you will have different schedules, different taste in music, food, TV, and more. Get a roommate that is close to your age.

GETTING ALONG WITH A ROOMMATE

1. *Don't sweat the small stuff* – If they leave the toilet seat up or forget to unload the dishwasher, don't lecture them about it.

2. *Don't use their stuff unless you have permission* – It was always annoying to see a roommate wear something of mine when they didn't even ask.

3. *Return their stuff after you borrow it* – If you do borrow something, return it in a timely manner. If it was clothes, wash or dry clean them before you return them.

4. *Don't eat their food* – This can cause fights. When you are struggling to meet all your financial obligations, food is like money. If you eat your roommate's food, it is like stealing their money.

5. *Assign tasks or rotate tasks* – Have one person assigned to garbage detail while the other unloads the dishwasher, then switch next month.

6. *Make a serious effort to get along* – Try to get along. Don't just give up when you have a small disagreement.

7. *Do activities together* – If you become active together, there is a better chance of becoming friends.

8. *Become friends* – It is easier to get along when you enjoy each other's company and take into account the other person's feelings.

9. *Watch stuff on TV you both agree on* – No one likes a "Remote Hog".

10. *Clean up after yourself* – This includes your dishes, your clothes, and your messes. Notice the word "your." If everyone cleaned up after themselves it would be so much easier.

6. Family and Marriage Tips
Family Tips

1. *Stop asking for money* – Sooner or later your money bank will go dry, or worse, they will hold it against you.

2. *Enjoy the time you spend with family* – Your family will always be there for you through good times and bad. Come back from college to visit. They miss you, and a better relationship will be formed because they have learned to let go, and you have become more mature.

3. *Enjoy the time spent away from family* – Sometimes your family can drive you crazy. It is nice to take a break and become more independent from your family. But remember #2.

4. *Value their opinion* – Your family cares about you more than anyone else, and they also know you better than anyone else. They may know what is better for you than you know yourself.

5. *Do what is best for you* – Although you value their opinion, they are not in your shoes. Listen to your family, but do what is best for you.

6. *Learn to accept them* – You can't change families. Learn to love them in all shapes and characteristics.

7. *Don't over extend yourself to your family* – Some family members are selfish and they will use the fact that you are family to take advantage of you and gain something they want. If your cousin has a gambling problem and needs a loan to repay some debt, don't give it to him just because you're family. It will only cause tension.

8. *Be more positive than negative* – It is much easier to see the negative things in your family than to see the positive things. Even through hard times, positive aspects can keep a struggling family together.

9. *Expect to not make all your family members happy* – All your family members care for each other but everyone is very different. Decisions and activities that involve your family will leave some family members happy and others unhappy. Try to find a common ground or do what makes you happy.

10. *Make the effort to spend time with them when you can* – Life is too short and too many things can happen. Take the weekend and go visit your grandparents or an aunt and uncle.

GETTING MARRIED

1. *Wait till one of you graduates* – It is easier to pay off wedding debt when one of you has a good steady income.

2. *Go through pre-marriage counseling* – A good marriage counselor will show you all the negative aspects of getting married. If you survive that without breaking up, you are probably right for each other.

3. *Start planning early* – Get as much done as early as possible. There will be less stress during that last couple of weeks of planning.

4. *Budget yourself and your soon-to-be spouse* – Don't allow each other to go overboard on costs. Spend the extra money on your honeymoon.

5. *Allow at least 8 months after the engagement* – This still gives plenty of time to reserve the church, send out invitations, buy and reserve wedding apparel, and more.

6. *Don't sweat the small stuff* – It is a given that things will happen that are out of your control. Stay focused on what is most important.

7. *Find people that can help* – If you have an aunt that bakes cakes or your uncle that has a condo in Malibu, use the resources available.

8. *Try to keep yourself happy instead of everyone else* – The wedding is your day to celebrate. Most people might not even go to the reception that you have spent thousands of dollars on. All the leftovers are a waste of money.

9. *Work on the plans together* – Include each other in the wedding plans, even if one of you makes most of the decisions, at least tell the other about it. Remember it is a celebration for both of you.

10. *Expect the unexpected* – It might rain, the limo might break down, and your drunk uncle might show up.

7. Studying, Finals, Food, & More
Ways to study and do well in classes

1. *Set the right atmosphere* – No distractions, comfortable desk and chair, etc....

2. *Take notes and review them* – Review your notes before class and after class, even rewrite or type your notes to absorb the material better.

3. *Develop a schedule* – Write down your test and assignment dates, and set time aside for studying.

4. *Use learning aids* – Flash cards, diagrams, chapter outlines, formula sheets, etc.

5. *Go to class and listen* – It is one thing to just go to class. Participate, stay awake, and you will absorb more from the lecture.

6. *Be interested in the topics* – I know it is hard to be interested in taking the anti-derivative of a calculus equation, but do your best.

7. *Study with someone who is better at the subject than you* – They can help you through the rough spots, also they gain in understanding. See #8.

8. *Study with someone who does not know the topic as well as you* – When you explain the topic to them, it helps you learn and retain the material better.

9. *Take a 10 minute break for every hour of study* – If you take a break to readjust your focus, it will be helpful in retaining the information.

10. *Visit the instructor to get help or ask a general question* – You would be surprised the effect of visiting an instructor will have on your grade. They see that you are making an effort and that may make a difference when you are on that 'B' to 'C' border.

ALTERNATIVES TO READING THE WHOLE CHAPTER

1. *Attend class and take notes* – Most professors will test you on topics covered in class lectures. Study your notes from these lectures and use your book to look up key points.

2. *Do the end of the chapter review questions* – I have had professors that included the same questions on the test. It also doesn't hurt to do them because it is just practice.

3. *Make an outline hitting key terms and points* – Skim through the chapter and write down key points and topics. It is easier to study a 2 to 3 page outline compared to a 30 page chapter.

4. *Study examples or case studies* – This is where I learned the most, especially in classes that involve problem solving. A math book can talk forever about taking a derivative, but an example is worth 100 pages of text.

5. *Read the chapter review* – Key points, vocabulary, and other very useful information will help you.

6. *Get a used book that has highlighted sections* – I have looked for and bought used books that have highlighted sections, answered review questions, and key notes in the margins. This may let you know what professors find most important.

7. *Highlight key sections while the instructor lectures* – Some professors follow the book so closely that if you were to take notes you would be copying the book. Just bring your book and highlight sections covered.

8. *Look up the author's website* – Most books make use of the internet and place overheads, review notes, and more on the publisher's website. Look in the appendix or preface in the textbook to find the web address.

9. *Get the study guide* – Some text books offer a review/study guide book or a solutions manual. The extra cost may be very worth while.

10. *Use your syllabus* – Many professors give a semester outline with the syllabus. Make sure to study every topic.

Tips to Stay Organized

1. *Use a planner* – Write down your homework due dates, tests dates, and other important information.

2. *Look at your syllabus* – Pay attention to the dates and stay on top of things.

3. *Post-it Notes* – Little reminders to stick anywhere.

4. *5-subject notebook* – One notebook that has a section for each class will help you keep things together.

5. *Folder for each class* – Keep all your papers for a class in one folder.

6. *Monthly calendar* – Look at the whole month in one view. Mark important days.

7. *PDA* – Personal Data Assistant. Include dates, addresses, notes, and more. The new ones have Word, Excel, and Outlook.

8. *Write notes on your hand* – Quick self-reminders about something that you don't want to forget.

9. *Have a place for everything* – Leave your keys in one place, your school books in another, and more. If you leave your things in the same place then you won't lose things and be rushed when you are trying to find them.

10. *Your computer* – Use MS Outlook or Yahoo personal planner.

WAYS TO STAY AWAKE IN CLASS

1. *Caffeine, Caffeine, Caffeine* – When all else fails.

2. *No Caffeine* – Your body may become too dependent on it and after that caffeine rush is gone you will become tired again.

3. *Do something* – Take notes, doodle, keep active to stay awake, but always listen.

4. *Get at least 6 hours of sleep* – Ensures you have had enough sleep to make it through the day.

5. *Sleep no longer than 8-9 hours* – If you oversleep, you can end up more tired than energized.

6. *Eat right* – Eat enough servings of fruits and vegetables with your normal helpings of proteins, carbohydrates, and essential fats.

7. *Exercise Regularly* – If you stay active in life, you will have more energy throughout the day.

8. *Force yourself to listen* – The lecture may be very boring, but try to listen and retain the information.

9. *Stay active in the lecture* – Ask questions, read from the book, or write notes.

10. *Go to the restroom* – Get up and get some blood flowing; splash some water on your face in the restroom.

Tips to make it through your finals in one piece

1. *Prepare way before finals week* – You should be studying the whole semester. Staying on top of your schoolwork will make it easier during finals week.

2. *Relax and don't stress* – If it comes down to it, you can always repeat the class or take a "B" instead of the "A" you wanted.

3. *Study old tests from semesters before* – Find someone that has taken the class before you and get copies of their old exams. Even if they will not be the same test, it is great practice.

4. *Take time off from work* – If your job allows it, take a few days off to concentrate on studying.

5. *Take breaks* – I don't know how many times I was stumped on figuring out the solution to a problem. When I came back to it later, it seemed so much clearer.

6. *Study with people smarter than you* – They can teach you and it helps both of you learn the material better.

7. *Ask the teacher any questions you have about material* – Many times, the professor will have a review session before the final. Don't just sit there, ask questions. More than likely, other students have the same questions, but are too afraid to ask.

8. *Get tutored* – If your school offers this as a free service, take advantage.

9. *Eat breakfast* – You can't concentrate when your stomach is growling.

10. *Get at least 6 hours of sleep a night* – I have been useless at finals when I stayed up most of the night studying. Your brain does not retain information when you are too tired.

TOP FOODS/MEALS TO SURVIVE THE FINALS WEEK

1. *Ramen noodles rule!* – Cheap, tasty, quick, easy. Need I say more?

2. *Hamburger Helper* – Pasta and meat in a tasty sauce. Cook the meat, add the contents of the box. Should be enough for 2 to 3 servings.

3. *Fruit* – Natural energy food for your body

4. *Pizza, Pizza, Pizza* – Delivery or DiGiorno.

5. *Subway* – Low fat, made your way, large selection, nice fast food alternative.

6. *Any 24-hour restaurant* – Sometimes when you have been studying for ten hours and it is 1:00 am, a road trip to a 24-hour diner will be worth it, and bring your book.

7. *Tuna fish* – Mayo and two pieces of bread. An instant sandwich with plenty of protein.

8. *Chef Boyardee* – Ravioli, Spaghetti, and other tasty pastas in a can. Open and nuke them for two minutes.

9. *Frozen chicken nuggets* – Microwave, toaster oven, or if you are really hard up defrost them by putting some foil around them and leaving them in the sun for a while. Hey. The chicken is already cooked!

10. *Sliced meats* – Make yourself a good sandwich and grab some chips and salsa.

8. Automobiles
Top car tips

1. *Change your oil* – Every 3,000 miles. You would be amazed at how long this will keep your car going.

2. *Invest in an alarm* – Even a cheap alarm with a flashing red light will deter a thief from breaking into your car.

3. *Wash the bird droppings off ASAP* – I learned this the hard way. If you leave bird droppings on your car too long, it will eat away at the clear coat and paint.

4. *Keep up with regular scheduled maintenance* – Injector cleaning, transmission service, tune-ups, and more. See the owner's manual.

5. *Clean your car* – Keeps it looking nice and it boosts the resale value.

6. *Wax it at least twice a year* – Preserves your paint to keep the car looking its best.

7. *Rotate your tires every 6,000 miles* – The tread will wear evenly and the tires will last longer.

8. *Don't drive your car like it is a NASCAR race car* – Don't power shift; don't floor it; don't over extend your car. Most likely your car is not a Corvette, therefore, it is not made to be driven like a race car.

9. *Inspect your car every once in a while* – Check air in tires, check oil and other fluid levels, and pay attention to anything leaking.

10. *Keep an eye on your dashboard* – When the "Service Engine" light comes on, or your engine temperature is in the red, don't ignore it.

CAR BUYING TIPS

1. *Buy a car that is good on gas* – There is a big difference in spending $15 a week as compared to $30. It adds up.

2. *When in doubt buy a Honda or Toyota* – Both car manufacturers make a number of nice looking cars. Both brands are very reliable.

3. *Decide the role of your car* – Do you want to haul everyone around in your six-passenger SUV or would you rather ride with everyone else because you have a small two-seater?

4. *Do not buy new* – A brand new car depreciates so quickly that you can save a couple thousand by buying slightly used.

5. *Think reliability instead of style* – You are going to be busy with many things in college. Get a car that you are not going to worry about breaking down.

6. *Save up for the down payment, tax, tag, and title* – If you must finance your car, it is nice to have a down payment on a car. It will save you on monthly payments and total interest paid.

7. *Determine what you can afford every month* – What are your other financial obligations? How much money do you have left over after these obligations are met? This will help you determine what kind of car you can afford.

8. *Find someone to co-sign on the loan with you* – Someone that has a great credit history can get you a lower interest rate and you will gain some credit points. Respect their good faith; make your payments so you don't harm their good credit.

9. *Do your homework* – Carfax.com, Consumer Reports, and Kelley Blue Book. Find out the reliability, history, and value of the car.

10. *Negotiate the price* – After you have done your homework you are equipped to negotiate. Remember the numbers you came up with yourself and don't let the salesperson get too much out of you.

9. Health

Tips to Keeping Healthy

1. *Take vitamins* – This is an easy way to get your daily nutrients.

2. *Eat breakfast* – Your brain will work better and a light breakfast will jumpstart your metabolism.

3. *Take up a physical activity* – Do something you enjoy like basketball, jogging, swimming, or another activity.

4. *Get at least 6 hours of sleep a night* – Any less than that and you may be tired the rest of the day.

5. *Try to average 8 hours of sleep a night* – This is the optimal amount of sleep if you can get it.

6. *Wash your hands often* – This will help fight off a number of germs that are contracted through touching things with your hands.

7. *Drink water* – Your body needs water to survive. If you deplete your body's water supply, your health may suffer.

8. *Keep warm* – Your natural body temperature is 98.6 degrees. When it is 58.6 degrees outside, keep your body from dropping in temperature.

9. *Maintain a balanced diet* – I know this is hard when you are busy, but try. It will make a difference in your health, weight, and energy.

10. *Keep from stressing out* – Stressing out lowers your immune system's ability to protect your body from infection.

TIPS TO LOOSE THAT 15 POUNDS OR BEER GUT BY SPRING BREAK

1. *Instead of drinking Coke, drink water* – This cuts down about 140 calories per soft drink.

2. *Get a job that is physical* – Restaurant server, construction worker, landscaping, or others where you do something other than just sit or stand.

3. *Walk or ride a bike to class* – Instead of riding the bus or driving when you live less than a mile away from school. Find a more physically active way to get there.

4. *Use the stairs instead of the elevator* – If you use the stair climber in the gym, why not use the real thing when you get the chance?

5. *Start eating and drinking light* – Light dressing, soda, beer, and more. Usually tastes the same with fewer calories.

6. *Cut down on junk food* – Instead of fatty McDonalds, go for Subway.

7. *Napkin your pizza* – Use a napkin to soak up the excess grease on top of the pizza. This can cut down on many calories even though you are still eating pizza.

8. *Eat more fruits and vegetables instead of french fries and chips* – Fruits and vegetables burn off quicker and easier. Fatty carbohydrates don't break down as easily and are usually stored as reserved energy cells.

9. *Stop overeating* – When you're not hungry anymore, wrap up the rest of your dinner and take it home to eat for lunch tomorrow instead of trying to finish it off.

10. *Eat fewer calories than you burn off* – The bottom line is, consume less than your body uses in a given day.

Kick a Nagging Cold in a Week

1. *Vitamins* – C, Zinc, multi-vitamin, Echinacea. This over-the-counter combination fights the cold and strengthens your immune system. Please read the indications on the label and consult your physician.

2. *Drink lots of water* – Staying hydrated will help fight the cold.

3. *Cough drops* – They help you breathe and relieve a sore throat.

4. *Vicks Vapor Rub* – This helps you breathe easy at night.

5. *Nyquil* – Fights a cold while you sleep and helps you rest.

6. *Work up a sweat* – If you have a small cold and have enough energy, try to participate in some physical activity. Working up a sweat helps fight off the cold.

7. *Stay really warm* – Your body's temperature is important when fighting a cold.

8. *Eat something high in vitamin C* – Eat an orange or a grapefruit.

9. *Get plenty of rest* – Your body needs to rest to have the strength to fight off the cold.

10. *Take a hot bath* – The heat and steam will help you breathe and fight the cold.

10. Final Helpful Topics
Things to do your senior year in college

1. *Fill out a graduation application early* – The records office is not perfect. Get this done early and double check with them to ensure that everything is set for your graduation. Pay attention to required dates in your catalog.

2. *Attend job fairs and hand out your resume* – A great way to start networking by meeting potential employers.

3. *Collect references* – Make sure to get your favorite professors' contact information and reference letters if possible. Also, get past employers' contact information.

4. *Talk to your professors about job opportunities* – Usually professors are still in the loop of their professional work field and they have contacts out there looking for a new employee.

5. *Double check your graduation requirements* – Go through your requirements one last time to make sure you will graduate. Don't wait for the records office to let you

know. I got my letter of completion 2 days before I walked across the stage. Imagine if it had been a letter of incompletion, which happens often.

6. *Prepare yourself for an easier school load* – Take your harder classes 2 to 3 semesters before your last semester to have the best possible opportunity to graduate when you anticipate.

7. *Send out announcements* – This is a huge accomplishment; send out the announcements to let your family and friends know.

8. *Get fellow graduates' contact information* – Stay in contact with fellow graduates. Who knows? They may be good contacts in the future when you both work in similar fields.

9. *Increase your resume power* – Get a job or take a class to gain experience in something that will look great on your resume.

10. *When you cross the stage, celebrate* – It is time to relax. No more paying to go to class. Now you can go out and get paid.

TIPS TO LIVE BY IN ALL ASPECTS OF LIFE

1. *Don't procrastinate* – If you have time now, do it. If it is due soon, don't wait till the last moment. A lot of people are procrastinators. If you break the habit, then you will be better off.

2. *Enjoy life* – Be happy you are alive and that you make a difference in people's lives.

3. *Have faith* – Faith in God, faith in people you care about, and faith in yourself.

4. *Do what is best for you* – No one knows you like you know yourself.

5. *Keep in close touch with people you care about* – We meet so many people in our lives. Keep in touch with those that influenced your life, supported you, befriended you, and most of all, loved you.

6. *Treat everyone the way you would like to be treated* – Remember the Golden Rule.

7. *Don't judge people* – You truly don't know them and what they must go through daily.

8. *Think positively* – It is easier to see the negative in everything but remember, it can always be worse. Be grateful for what you have and what you can do.

9. *Give your best effort in all your actions* – If you don't give your best effort and fail, you will never know if you could have succeeded.

10. *Strive to be better* – In anything you do; to be a better Christian, a better student, a better boyfriend/girlfriend, a better roommate, etc....

WORD TO THE WISE

1. *Lost sleep is lost* – If you miss 4 hours one night, don't try to make it up the next night. If you oversleep, then you will be even more tired.

2. *Drink lots of water* – Your body is made up mostly of water. Keep it replenished.

3. *Eat a balanced diet* – This keeps you healthy and energized.

4. *Take a multi-vitamin everyday* – Quick easy way to get the minerals and nutrients your body needs.

5. *Wash your hands often* – Fights off germs that are contracted from touching things a lot of other people have touched.

6. *Don't overeat* – Eat until you have had a comfortable amount. If you overeat, your body will store the excess food as fat and you will become tired because your body is trying to digest all the food.

7. *Do a physical activity 2 or 3 times a week* – This keeps you energized and your metabolism up.

8. *Enjoy learning* – You will be doing it your whole life.

9. *Don't expect everything to go your way* – Stuff happens in our life that is beyond our control. Don't let it get you down.

10. *Enjoy life* – Have fun, accomplish goals, and cherish personal relationships.

You have brains in your head.

You have feet in your shoes.

You can steer yourself in any direction you choose.

You're on your own.

And you know what you know.

You are the person who'll decide where to go.

- Dr. Seuss

TOP COLLEGE COMEDY MOVIES

1. "Animal House"
2. "PCU"
3. "Van Wilder"
4. "Dead Man on Campus"
5. "Old School"
6. "Revenge of the Nerds"
7. "Threesome"
8. "Back to School"
9. "Senseless"
10. "How High"

TIPS TO GET OUT OF STUDENT LOAN DEBT

I will let you know. For now, try to take the least amount possible. Also, use the same lender for each loan, and take out subsidized loans only.

HELPFUL WEBSITES

www.mycollegetips.com - The home website for this book.

www.learningstart.com - A Complete Education Directory.

www.half.com - A great place to buy textbooks, CDs, DVDs, and more.

www.ebay.com - Because it is eBay.

www.priceline.com - Great for air plane tickets, hotels, car rentals, and more.

www.travelocity.com - Great for air plane tickets, hotels, car rentals, and more.

www.expedia.com - Great for air plane tickets, hotels, car rentals, and more.

www.hotwire.com - Great for air plane tickets, hotels, car rentals, and more.

www.fafsa.ed.gov - Free Application for Federal Student Aid Website.

www.nslds.ed.gov - National Student Loan Data System.

www.ecampus.com - A website for college textbooks, apparel, and merchandise.

www.supercollege.com - A website devoted to college students.

www.dontcopy.com - A website with 25,000+ term paper examples.

www.thesemester.com - A helpful tips website for college students.

www.campusblues.com - Many helpful articles about your college years.

www.campuscareercenter.com - Website devoted to employment for college students.

www.collegeclub.com - Buy college merchandise, read articles, do fun stuff.

ABOUT THE AUTHOR

James Scott Parker was born in Hixson, Tennessee. His family moved to Phoenix, Arizona when he was 5. James graduated from Westview High School in 1995, and he attended three colleges in three years before moving back to Hixson in August 1998. James then enrolled at the University of Tennessee at Chattanooga and changed his major. After eight straight years of college, James finally graduated in May of 2003 with a Bachelor of Science degree in Computer Science and a Minor in Entrepreneurship.

Today, James is married to his beautiful wife, Kalee, and he works full time at Tennessee Valley Authority as a Data Analyst. James plans on returning to college to get his masters degree in business. He is very creative by nature and is usually working on some entrepreneurial project. Please feel free to visit his personal website at www.jsparker.com to get more information about his current and/or past projects.

PRESENTATIONS AND SPECIAL EVENTS

The author is available for presentations to clubs, schools, youth groups, and other student related organizations. Mr. Parker is qualified to discuss his book, personal college experience, lessons learned, and most everything related to a college student's life. Please visit www.mycollegetips.com for more details and contact information.

TO ORDER MORE COPIES OF THIS BOOK

Order online at: www.mycollegetips.com

Order by mail: Send a check or money order payable to James S. Parker to:
1627 Roberson Road, Hixson, TN 37343 USA

NAME: _____

SHIPPING ADDRESS:_____

_____

CITY:_____ ST/PROV.: _____ ZIP: _____

EMAIL ADDRESS (optional) _____

_____ (quantity) @ $9.95 US or $12.95 (Canada) =   _____

Tennessee residents please include an additonal $.92 each for TN sales tax. _____

SHIPPING and handling: Please include $3.50 for one book.   _____

For larger orders please see the website or inquire by mail for reduced
shipping charges and quantity discounts.   TOTAL _____

INTERESTED IN ADVERTISING IN THIS BOOK?
INTERESTED IN ADVERTISING ON THE
ACCOMPANYING WEBSITE?

Please visit the website for possible advertising opportunities to reach the "College Student Market."

www.mycollegetips.com

Layout and design: Karen Paul Stone
Text in Bachelor Pad and Baker Signet on Cougar 60# white